Marjorie & Ernie Wanless
19 May 1976
1973
$10-
indexed

W9-BMH-565

THE BANDS CANADIANS DANCED TO

ACKNOWLEDGEMENTS

A special vote of thanks to the bandleaders who took valuable time to recall dates, places and incidents; to Harry Houston, a man with a prodigious memory and likewise Bill Baker, Edna Bedlington, Lloyd Boddison, Mrs. Gordon Braund, Nat Cassels, Ed Culley, Gerry Dunn, Vern Graham, Barney Krivel, Bert Meachin, Reef McGarvey, Rita Romanelli, Dunc Snider, Stan Pederson, Norm Thompson, Homer Watson and researcher Marie Oldham, who all dug happily back into the past to tell us about the bands Canadians danced to...

designed by Michel Socha

THE BANDS CANADIANS DANCED TO

—◇—

Helen McNamara & Jack Lomas

GRIFFIN HOUSE
TORONTO 1973

THE ONTARIO HISTORICAL SOCIETY

© Helen McNamara and Jack Lomas 1973

ISBN 0 88760 063 8

Published by Griffin Press Limited
455 King Street West, Toronto,
Canada M5V 1K7

All rights reserved. No part of this book may
be reproduced, transmitted in any form or by
any means, electronic, mechanical, photocopy-
ing, recording or otherwise, or stored in a re-
trieval system without the written permission
in advance of the publisher.

Printed and bound in Canada
by T. H. Best Printing Company Limited
Don Mills, Ontario

FOREWORD

BUT HELEN...JACK...You didn't mention Al Wright and his Night Hawks, Cal Temple and his Tantalizing Toe-Ticklers, or Elwood Glover and his Campus Boys! The year was 1932. The city was Moose Jaw, Saskatchewan and the local airways were limited to 250 watts of unfettered power from CHAB, which on a clear night could be heard as far as Gravelburg!

This book is an absolute gem....I received a letter from a viewer recently, a student who had an essay assignment, thought the Canadian jazz scene would be an appropriate subject and would I give her the benefit of my experience. I was stunned....A Canadian jazz scene? I couldn't remember there had ever been one. But then when your invitation came to do this foreword I began to think: Our jazz scene meant dancing, and dancing meant bands which as you so ably state, were the life blood of inexpensive radio entertainment during four decades of a world long gone.

I can honestly state, the dance band has been the raison d'etre for most of my life. From the days of the crystal set in the twenties to a recent radio series I've been doing for the CBC, "Echoes of an Era", the dance band has been my fondest hobby. Whereas the guitar is now the instrumental choice of every budding matinee idol, the alto saxophone was the thing in my day (Rudy Vallee was the Presley of his time.) My favourite musicians were Rudy Weidoeft, Andy Senella, Freddie Gardner and the Six Brown Brothers. I longed for the day when I could sit in a sax section surrounded by every instrument in the woodwind family (no doubt inspired by a picture of Ross Gorman of the Paul Whiteman band.) The brief fling I had in my latter student days playing school dances, the Oddfellow's Hall and the Tuesday Night Young Peoples' in the basement of St. John's church, revealed to me two truths about the dance band business: That it's a lifetime dedication if you were to succeed and that I hadn't the talent to become really good. So, a new phase in my life began...radio...

Radio was the ideal solution. I could be near the music I loved and perhaps in some way share with others what I thought was one of life's greatest pleasures.

The late night dance remote was almost the Nemesis of my education years. Against dire parental warnings of destined oblivion I would devour the dance band remote from what was the geographic centre of radio reception for North America. My radio would bring in everything from WEAF and 'JZ in New York to WLW Cincinnati in the east, to KOA Denver, KPO San Francisco and KFI-KNX Los Angeles in the west. That meant everything from the Central Park Casino to the Beverly-Wiltshire Hotel, and my idols were the style bands: Hal Kemp, Freddy Martin, Orville Knapp, Wayne King, Jan Garber and Guy Lombardo (Ted Weems and Ben Bernie never had enough identity to suit me); the piano playing leaders like Eddie Duchin, Nat Brandwynne, Henry King and Carmen Cavallaro and the great ensemble bands of Isham Jones, Casa Loma and Dick Jurgens. But Chicago was the town: WGN, WBBM and WENR, all representing the three American networks, brought one a visual image of every dance emporium in the area. When I went to Chicago in '33 I knew exactly where to go, recognizing the places' decor immediately: The Aragon and Trianon Ballrooms, the Terrace Room of the Morrison Hotel with Frankie Masters, the Drake with Clyde McCoy, the Bismark with Art Kassel, the Sherman with Ben Bernie, the Via Lago Cafe with Herbie Kaye (whose girl singer was Dorothy Lamour), the Palmer House with Ted Weems, the Granada Cafe with Paul Whiteman and the Chez Paree with Henry Busse.

In western Canada, who could forget the Silvertone Seven in Regina, Leo Smuntan from Saskatoon, and a fabulous band from

North Dakota led by Harry Turner? Then there were the Mart Kenney broadcasts from Waterton Lake and the Hotel Saskatchewan; the bigtimers from Eastern Canada would come in: Jack Denny, Luigi Romanelli and Billy Bissett.

It wasn't until I arrived as a fledgling announcer with CBC Toronto that I suddenly found myself as dance band announcer for almost every remote in town. I was thrilled to find my services much in demand for these programs, but I soon learned the reason: All the other announcers hated them! But for me, just to be on speaking terms with the brothers Romanelli, Trump Davidson, Bert Niosi, Horace Lapp, Norman Harris, Ozzie Williams and Frank Bogart opened up a whole new world. There were also the great radio leaders: Percy Faith, Robert Farnon, Russ Gerow, Percy Pasternak, Samuel Hersenhoren, Paul Sherman, Simeon Joyce, Rex Battle and Johnny Burt (who conducted my own series back in the early fifties).

Toronto had its dance palaces where the famous would play their one-nighters: Cuthbert & Dellers' Palais Royale, the Palace Pier, Club Top Hat, the Silver Slipper and the Masonic Temple. The memorable CNE Tent where the big names would play and where I used to emcee the American network shows of Tommy Dorsey and Artie Shaw (the Old Gold Summer Show in the Fall of '39 with Artie Shaw's band, the four King Sisters and Warren Hull . . . wow!) Working with the Glenn Miller band on the Mutual network in 1942 during their Ontario tour was probably the highlight.

So you see, Helen and Jack, radio and records have been my life and until this book came along I never realized that I shared so much history. I salute you both. Fortunate was I to have experienced it and your readers are lucky to see it in its proper perspective.

You've shown and said it all.

Elwood Glover,
Toronto, June, 1973.

CONTENTS

'LET'S DANCE!'

Right from the outset I have to admit that my memories of Canadian dance bands in the thirties and forties are rather vague. While men such as Jack Lomas were dancing to the local bands I was caught up in the mystique of the visiting U.S. bands, those musical gypsies who periodically descended upon Toronto. Fortunately, we jazz fans were also hearing the house bands, and so in time, mostly because of the swinging sounds of the Bert Niosi band at the Palais Royale and Trump Davidson's band at the Palace Pier, we began listening to other Canadian bands.

Even if you never did get around to hearing the dance bands in person there were enough radio broadcasts to tell you where they played and how they played and that meant whether they were sweet or hot. And that was very important indeed! You came to know the names of Mart Kenney, Horace Lapp, Art Hallman, Ferde Mowry, Paul Firman, Frank Bogart, Ellis McLintock . . .

You wondered how it came about that Glen Gray's American band started out at Toronto's Casa Loma. If you were a jazz fan you wondered at the popularity of Guy Lombardo's Royal Canadians. Then years later, you might change your mind as I did when I met the gentleman and realized that his music, even after fifty years, means everything to him and whether you like it or not, disagree or not, he is an institution . . . a Canadian-born institution and that makes it even better.

1

We might as well face it. The Canadian dance band scene was always dominated by the better publicized Americans and we Canadians were all too ready to accept the Americans as the best on earth.

That's why it's something of a miracle that the Lombardos back in the twenties actually broke the barricade, to become in time the U.S.A.'s sweetest dance band. A miracle indeed . . . for the Canadian inferiority complex was fully in evidence in those far away days. Maybe it was the forties and the advent of World War II that began to change things.

The Canadians who went overseas heard many bands and perhaps came to realize that our musicians were equally accomplished. It was a belief already proved in the thirties when Billy Bissett took his band over to play in London's Savoy and Mayfair Hotels and Trump Davidson's band was whisked off by British bandleader Ray Noble for a two year tour of the British Isles. It was confirmed again when Denny Vaughan, the talented pianist-singer with Horace Lapp's orchestra during the forties stayed on in England after the war and became an idol of British teenagers.

I think most of us know now that Canadian musicians are among the best in the world and just like musicians in the United States and England and wherever dance bands played, some attracted more attention than others, some were just naturally more colourful, more aggressive, more magnetic. It is around them that the legends grow . . .

Talk to musicians and sooner or later some names, more than others, pop into the conversations. In Toronto that has to be the Romanellis.

(Apologies if Toronto is mentioned frequently but it can't be otherwise. Toronto, even in the twenties, was a focal point for Canadian musicians as New York was for Americans. Sooner or later many musicians, many dance bands, found their way to Toronto.)

But to get back to the Romanellis. Horace Lapp, for one, remembers them as charming people. "I always thought Luigi was a good fiddle player," he said. "He had a smooth, sentimental style."

Trump Davidson, a seven year veteran of the Luigi Romanelli orchestra, admired the leader's talent for hiring the right people. One important man who came out of that band was Percy Faith, who before he went to Hollywood won national recognition for his CBC programs, including one called Music By Faith, a title that so baffled a politician, so it is said, that he thought it was a new CBC program on religion. Most of the Romanelli arrangements were written by Percy Faith, Harry Ginzler or Trump Davidson.

"Luigi was always changing the style of the band," said Trump.

Guy Lombardo and the Orchestra in 1932.

"He'd hear a broadcast or a recording by Isham Jones or maybe Hal Kemp and go back to the hotel and scrap his current library."

Luigi, who spent 20 years as a leader at the King Edward Hotel, had a hotel room filled with music and a librarian in charge. It was said that the library, valued at $50,000 and his Stradivarius violin were among his most prized possessions.

Besides his King Edward Hotel orchestra, Luigi would sometimes appear with the Romanelli orchestras sent out to other ballrooms on weekend dates, but it was an expensive honour.

Said Trump: "When we played at the King Edward we'd quit at 1.30 a.m., then go on to the Hunt Club or a debutante dance and play for hours. To have Luigi appear with the band, they'd pay him $1,000."

The well-paid Romanelli musicians, an exclusive group that at one time or another included Horace Lapp, who later led his own orchestra, and arranger-composer Johnny Burt, sometimes made as much as $100 a week, a huge salary for depression days. Sometimes they played non-stop. As Trump recalls those hectic years: "When Eaton's College Street Store opened in the fall of 1930 we played three sessions a day on the main floor, then went on to the King Edward from 10.30 p.m. to 1.30 a.m. We did the same thing when the Bank of Commerce on King street opened the same year."

The entrance to the King Edward Hotel in the years when Luigi Romanelli's orchestra was the star attraction in the Oak Room.

The King Edward Hotel as it appeared in the thirties.

Canada Steamship Lines
*The Cayuga...a romantic re-
minder of the twenties and thirties...
was famous for its moonlight dance
cruises on Lake Ontario.*

*The Don Romanelli musicians
ham it up in another picture taken on
the popular Lake Ontario ship, the
Cayuga, in the late twenties. Nat
Cassels is the young man playing
clarinet.*

Nat Cassel's memories go back even farther. As one of Toronto's top musicians he played clarinet and saxophone in Don Romanelli's band on the popular lake boat cruises as far back as 1918. In 1923, Nat joined brother Luigi's band, and then because he was a much-in-demand sideman moved to Detroit where he worked for several orchestras including the Seymour Simons band which featured a young alto sax player, Spike Knoblaugh, later known as Glen Gray.

For three or four years Nat was a member of Alexander's Ragtime Band, another Detroit outfit that hung out at Luigi's Cafe, not to be confused with Toronto's Luigi. The cafe, says Nat in his succinct fashion, was nothing more or less than 'a glorified blind pig.'

Glen Gray and the Casa Loma Orchestra. At Gray's right are Sonny Dunham and Pee Wee Hunt. At Gray's left, singer Kenny Sargent, Canadian-born trombonist Murray McEachern (extreme right, front row) who had left for the States in 1936 to play in Benny Goodman's orchestra joined the Glen Gray band in 1938.

It was the kind of place in those prohibition years when the elite, in gowns and tails, descended around 11 p.m. apparently to hear the band but more likely to look over the cluster of gangsters seated around a large table in a corner of the cafe. Lurid though their reputations were the gangsters were lavish donors to the musical arts. "They used to toss tips on the floor," said Nat. "Then a cigarette girl would come along, sweep up the money and split it with the six men in the band."

Nat consequently found himself pulling in a weekly salary of $75, plus $50 sweepings. When he travelled home to Toronto in the summer months, he had a quick rejoinder when Luigi asked him to come back to his band at his former $75 a week. "Why?" Nat would say. That usually ended the conversation.

On these trips home, Nat found himself a star. One time he appeared at the Auditorium, at Queen and Cowan streets, that

Toronto's Casa Loma where Canadians have danced in its fabulous ballrooms 40 years or more.

was publicized as the ballroom with the largest dance floor in Toronto. There Nat was billed as The Saxophone Wizard with his orchestra from Detroit. The price of admission: 75 cents for gents; 50 cents plus tax for the ladies.

"It was a big thing to be acclaimed in the States in those days," said Nat, but added that it was a pleasant way to be greeted in his home town. Even more pleasant were the boat dances which he continued to work in the thirties. One of the most popular was the boat that sailed daily at 5.25 p.m., loaded with office workers who dined on sandwiches and danced all the way across the lake to Queenston and back until the boat docked at 11.25 p.m.

Another Toronto musician with memories of the far away days is Edwin Culley of the famous Culley Brothers. He, too, played on the boats and when he speaks of the Cayuga and the Chippewa headed across the lake on balmy summer nights, passengers drenched in moonlight and the sounds of music ("The tunes? Oh, something like Sweet Leilani . . . ") floating up from the lounge, there is a longing to see and hear it all just the way it was.

Loren Cassina and his Orches- at a six-day bicycle race at Ma Leaf Gardens in the mid-thirti Second from left is Len Duke, w later became a bandleader. On his is trumpeter Jimmy Reynolds w shortly afterward joined Jack Hylto band in England.

But those days are gone and Ed Culley is a realistic man. During the war he worked at DeHavilland Aircraft plant and there he stayed for 30 years because in many ways it offered a security that would be difficult to find in the dance band business. He still played in the dance bands, though. He'd never be able to give up music because he knew it was important to him personally and to others. It was during the war years that he made that discovery.

One day he received a call asking him if he would play a Promenade Symphony concert, but he turned it down because he felt it wouldn't be right to give up his work at the war plant. A few hours later Culley was called to the office of the managing director and listened in astonishment when he was told that he must play in the concert. "Musicians are hard to get and it's wartime," said the director. "People must have music. They need you."

Culley went. It was his first symphony date and he enjoyed it, but dance band jobs were more to his liking. Early in his career he, too, had worked for Luigi Romanelli; he had appeared in Glen Gray's original band at Casa Loma and he had also spent a few months with Fred Waring's Pennsylvanians which for several years featured his brothers Fred and George Culley.

His very first job had been with Gilbert Watson's band at the Sunnyside Pavilion where he earned $22 a week. With that same band he recalls an unforgettable incident that took place one Sunday afternoon at Centre Island. The band was playing a concert at Gin's Pavilion, a nickel-a-dance place on the main street, and Culley happened to see three men staring at him. "It turned out that one of them was a trumpet player who had worked in the Waring band with my brother and then had gone on to Jean Goldkette's band. My brother, Fred, had told him to go see his kid brother when he got to Toronto. And there he was . . . a Goldkette musician . . . three Goldkette musicians, in fact . . . on Centre Island wanting to talk to me!"

Put it all together . . . incidents such as Culley and Cassels describe . . . the afternoons at the island, the moonlit nights on Lake Ontario, the carefree crowds in the great hotel ballrooms and the dance halls along the lakeshore, and the dance band broadcasts . . . put it all together and something begins to take shape: The Canadian dance band scene.

It was happening all over the country. Toronto was a hustling, bustling town even in the thirties but "hog town" didn't have a monopoly on the dance bands . . . thanks to radio.

In 1930 some 12 million American families owned radio sets. Canadians, comparatively speaking, weren't doing too badly. When the Canadian Radio Broadcasting Commission was formed in 1932 there were 600,000 receiving sets in Canada.

Most of the radio stations were centred in Toronto and Montreal. Some picked up U.S. network broadcasts, which, happily for music fans, meant that it was possible to hear the best of the big bands. Luckily, it was not always a one way route. Many Canadian orchestras were picked up by the U.S. Networks for broadcast in the United States.

Art Hallman (left), Bobby Gim by and Mart Kenney at an RCA Victor Record company autograph ing party in the wartime forties.

What was more important, though Canadians probably did not realize it at the time, was the emphasis that the CRBC, which became the Canadian Broadcasting Corporation in 1936, put on home grown talent. The Mart Kenney band, for one, broadcasting from Vancouver, became known from coast to coast in the thirties.

Mart Kenney's orchestra at the Royal York Hotel in 1939.

Mart Kenney's orchestra plays for Navy personnel at Saint John, N. B., on a Coca Cola Victory parade broadcast during the war years.

Radio, as Mart himself often remarked, was the making of his band. It helped quite a few others as well. Radio during the depression years offered ideal entertainment. The jobless were hardly in a position to go dancing but they still managed, with the help of radio programs, to listen to the tunes of the times, of which Brother Can You Spare A Dime was particularly pertinent.

In retrospect, the thirties was a golden era for musicians and fans. It was a time when "live" music was given a preference to recorded music on the airwaves. Bandleaders, in fact, preferred to be heard on radio rather than recordings.

Looking back it may seem strange that the dance band business reached its greatest heights during the depths of the depression, but one can understand why it happened.

Just as today's multi-forms of entertainment allow us to escape the pressures of this age, so entertainment in the thirties gave men and women a chance to forget, momentarily at least, the frustrations of unemployment, the degradation of poverty.

Radio could not have happened at a better time. The depression, triggered by the great Wall Street crash of October, 1929, had created a new way of life. To thousands of unemployed it was difficult enough to find money to pay the rent and grocery bills, let alone seek entertainment. Radio provided the magical answer, with hours of airtime devoted to comedy and music, soap operas and plays, to news and commentaries. It was possible to find all the entertainment one could desire without even stepping outside the home.

To those who lived in cities, it was a boon. To those who lived in rural areas, and one thinks especially of the vast expanse of the prairies, the radio not only provided entertainment and information, but gave to many Canadians a feeling of comradeship. Whereas entertainment, before radio, had been restricted to the vaudeville theatres and the ballrooms and the concert halls, now it was funnelled simultaneously into homes across the land . . . and best of all, without cost.

And yet, while thousands kept a nightly tryst beside their sets, it was a time of contrasts. Even though many were poor, money still flowed. (The Royal York Hotel, built just before the beginning of the depression, became a popular dance spot where patrons flocked to the Roof Garden and the Imperial Room. The cover charge was $2, a quite considerable sum for the times.)

The dance bands played no small part in alleviating the boredom and the hopelessness of the depression days. Oddly enough few songs touched upon the tribulations of the thirties. It was a time instead for foolishness (of which The Music Goes Round And Round in 1935 and Flat Foot Floogey With The Floy Floy in 1938 were typical examples) but it was a period that also produced more durable material, such as The Lady Is A Tramp, Have You Met Miss Jones and September Song.

By 1939, a year that was marked by a Royal Visit in the spring and the declaration of World War II in the fall, Canadians were talking about a ballad called I'll Never Smile Again, written by Toronto's Ruth Lowe and eventually recorded by Tommy Dorsey's orchestra. But in keeping with the times, the top seller of the

Ferde Mowry's orchestra poses with RCAF members after the band appeared at Manning Depot in October, 1945.

The Modernaires in a war-time setting. Note silhouettes of Franklin Delano Roosevelt and Winston Churchill along with the V for Victory sign.

year was the Beer Barrel Polka. Like The White Cliffs of Dover, Til Reveille and I Left My Heart At The Stage Door Canteen, it was to remain popular until the end of the war. (Still, the war years did produce some classics: The Last Time I Saw Paris, White Christmas, Swinging On A Star, It Might As Well Be Spring.)

The end of the big bands would come in the late forties but during the war the dance orchestras played a tremendous part in keeping up morale. An American radio survey showed that dance bands were first in popularity, well ahead of news, sports and variety shows. The sweet dance tunes rated far above the swing arrangements. Sentimental songs were the hit songs.

Dancing to the bands was an ideal way to relax. Fortunately for Canadians, the CBC continued to program all kinds of music, quite likely far more "live" music than it does today. Not only did Canadians hear their favourite Canadian bands but the CBC also made available network broadcasts from NBC, CBS and Mutual in the U.S.A.

But, as some veteran broadcasters will tell you, dance band broadcasts had been a way of life long before the war started. Bill Baker, an engineer with CFRB since the twenties, says it was in 1928 that all the stations started broadcasting. "And a dance band program was a good fill," he said. "The station didn't have to pay any money and a program meant free publicity for the ballroom." But all this eventually changed. "Later the bands started charging $2 a man."

CFRB's Saturday Night Around The Town broadcast was great for dancing. Said Baker: "We'd pick up bands at the Club Embassy, the King Edward and Royal York Hotels, the Old Mill, the Silver Slipper. We'd have engineers covering a couple of ballrooms, an announcer in each one and we'd broadcast from two to three hours, hopping from one place to another."

And so Canadians danced to the bands. They listened to them on radio and in the ballrooms. At home they could dance for hours and if they were in the money, drink a beer or sip wine, all this without an admission fee. Yet the dance halls were surprisingly busy.

Ask Jack Lomas. As a young man growing up in the depression (he was an east end Torontonian who hung around Fallingbrook Pavilion and the Balmy Beach Club) he wanted to be a musician and even went so far as to buy a trumpet and practise it. Eventually he came to realize that the musicians he was listening to were born to their profession (men such as Danny Perri and Jimmy Reynolds and Murray McEachern) and he might just as well sit back, relax and enjoy their music.

Frank Driggs photo
Isham Jones and his orchestra broadcast from the Ambassador Hotel in Atlantic City on Station WPG over the Columbia Broadcasting System.

Only Jack didn't sit still. From his early teens he had been visiting the dance halls, listening to the bands. He continued to do so. Needless to say he was most impressed by the Romanellis, particularly Luigi's band at the King Edward Hotel, and Luigi, it so happened must have had a soft spot for the 16 year old kid who kept turning up at the Oak Room entrance hoping he could get inside and listen to the orchestra in person.

Well, hotel managements weren't so lenient in those days and Lomas was banished. It wasn't too long, though, before he found himself listening to the band. Somehow he managed to meet Luigi and the maestro himself told Jack that he could sit up on the balcony, discreetly screened by a pillar or a drape, where he could look down and listen to the band unobserved.

Jack never forgot that experience, one that he ranks alongside the first time he heard the Isham Jones Orchestra. That was when he was 14 years old, a momentous age, because that's when he started collecting photos, some bartered, some bought, but all of them an invaluable documentation of the dance bands of yester-year.

The dance bands intrigued Jack so much that he would have liked to travel around and hear them all. (Many years later he did make a pilgrimage to the great ballrooms in the U.S.A. but that was a rather sad journey. The ballrooms in most of the hotels in New York and Chicago were empty and silent, opened only for private parties, for weddings and bar mitzvahs. But at least, he says gratefully, in those rooms rock 'n' roll never replaced the dance bands.)

He enjoys listening to dance bands now as much as when he first heard the Isham Jones broadcasts. "I used to hear the orchestra when it broadcast from the Ambassador Hotel in Atlantic City every Saturday afternoon. During the program they dropped a microphone off the end of the pier and you could hear the ocean roar and the band playing and I was completely caught up with it."

Years later Jack discovered that those memorable broadcasts originated in Ocean Studio, built by Station WPG at the end of Atlantic City's famous Steel Pier. It was from that nautical style studio (decorated like a ship with port holes, ship's bell and even a small lifeboat) that the microphone was lowered over the side of the pier to bring the roar of the waves to listeners along the CBS network.

Shortly after Jack discovered the Isham Jones band he wrote away to the leader asking for a photo. A picture was promptly sent to him, one that he greatly prizes. In the personnel is a clarinetist who was to take over the band when Jones gave it up in 1936. The clarinetist was Woody Herman.

Today there are signs that many Canadians of Jack Lomas' generation share his nostalgic yearnings. As the pace of life quickens there is an almost frantic endeavour to recapture the essence of life of forty, thirty, even twenty years ago. Not surprisingly the middle generation looks back upon the days of its youth with greatest favour, to the time when its music and its dances were of supreme importance. Somehow the music they heard and the way they danced typified those long ago decades: The Charleston, the Black Bottom, the Varsity Drag of the wildly prosperous twenties; the sedate waltzes and fox trots, the gliding tangos, the romping rhumbas of the thirties, a curious mixed-up period that also produced the Lindy Hop, the Big Apple and the Shag, dances that prevailed right into the forties, when servicemen and their girls filled the hotel ballrooms and dance halls, bodies flailing and gyrating, making a kind of acrobatic, if futile protest, against the madness of the times.

Some twenty-five years later the Twist arrived . . . a 'don't

Universal Films
Mary Tyler Moore and Julie Andrews as roaring twenties flappers in Thoroughly Modern Milie.

16

touch me, let me dance my own way' dance that was in its own way a perfect summation of the sixties, a dance adored by adolescents, adopted by the twenties and cautiously approached by the more athletic of their elders. Most of the middle-aged generation, however, will tell you that they prefer the dances of their youth, a fact that was readily evident in recent years when Bert Niosi and Trump Davidson re-assembled their bands for special reunion appearances. In both cases the bobby soxers of the forties were out in full force.

Even more enthusiastic about the current wave of nostalgia is Art Hallman, one of the few bandleaders of old who still runs a band, appearing regularly at Oshawa's Jubilee Pavilion which happens to be one of the few dance halls of old still open to the public. Hallman, who introduced his first band in 1944 at Casa Loma (an establishment that now caters only to private parties) still concentrates on swing era arrangements. He has found that the Jubilee audience, for the most part in the 40 to 60 year old age bracket, prefers the Glenn Miller-style songs. String of Pearls and In The Mood are a nightly must.

Jubilee owner Owen McCrohan prevailed upon Hallman to bring in his band for a one night stand in 1969. The response was so overwhelming with patrons coming from as far as 60 miles

Universal Films
The way flappers and their boy friends looked and danced in the twenties in a scene from Thoroughly Modern Millie. Julie Andrews and James Fox are the dancers.

away, that Hallman and his band (which includes such excellent sidemen as Ace Howard, Gordon Evans and Bobby Van Evera) have played there ever since.

Hallman finds it all very gratifying, citing the Jubilee for its happy, healthy atmosphere and evoking memories of the days "before TV when people entertained themselves by going out to shows or dances." It brings back the days when as a young man out in British Columbia he was very much a part of the dance band scene. And when he, like other westerners, such as his one time boss, Mart Kenney, or Barney Krivel, ex-musician, now manager of Casa Loma, talk of the west the Canadian dance band scene begins to come into focus.

It's then you begin to realize the tremendous part that dance bands played in this country, in the west as well as the east. When the bands played in dozens of small towns across the prairies and in the mountains and along the Pacific . . . bands like the Silvertone Seven from Saskatoon, the Art Harmony Seven, Les Crane and His Canadians, the orchestras of Len Chamberlain, Lafe Cassidy . . . the Brown Brothers . . . and Tantalizing Joe Tucker

Wide World Photo
Youngsters show how to jitterbug, popular in the forties and fifties.

18

Wide World Photo
Teenagers doing the Bunny Hop in 1957.

Wide World Photo
The Twist, a dance that swept the country in the early sixties.

19

Playing Popular Pieces and Pleasing Particular People . . .

Not all the bands in the west played in the dance halls. Boat cruises were big attractions in the twenties when ships sailed up and down the coast between Vancouver and Skagway. That was in Prohibition days, a time when many of the passengers were actually incognito celebrities, movie stars included, who liked to come up to Canada to enjoy the scenery and good Canadian whiskey.

All the dizzy events that hit the east in the depression were reflected in the west. In the very early days of the Mart Kenney band, one of its assignments was playing music for a marathon dance, one of those depressing events (that somehow fitted the depression) wherein contestants danced — or walked — until they collapsed.

And there were nights when the Kenney band wondered where all the people were, but that, of course, was long before it had swept to national fame with the help of radio broadcasts. By the time the war had arrived the crowds were turning out in thousands to hear the band from the west. It was the same everywhere. In Montreal the Forum was jammed with 2,000 people. In Winnipeg, the band played two one-night stands and seven thousand fans turned up.

But then Winnipeg was always a good dance band city. Barney Krivel, for one, says it was a hotbed of good musicians. Just outside the city there were dozens of 'bottle places' where the liquor was kept under the table, places where crowds congregated and crowds wanted music. Paul Grosney, who had his own band there, although in later years (at the Rancho Don Carlos from 1948 to 1958) looks upon Winnipeg as one of Canada's leading entertainment centres, where dance bands, radio programs and night clubs flourished. At the Don Carlos, the headliners included Bob Hope, Doris Day, Peggy Lee, Lena Horne, Liberace, Sophie Tucker.

Across the country, in the thirties and forties, the bands thrived. In Montreal the big names were Charlie Dornberger, Jack Denny, Louis Metcalfe, Earl Melloway, and Johnny Holmes, who featured a young pianist called Oscar Peterson and a trumpeter called Maynard Ferguson.

A great many musicians who made their way to Toronto were westerners but they came from the east as well. Perhaps the best known in Toronto today is Cy McLean, who was born in Sydney, Nova Scotia, and after he had arrived in the city, at 16 years of age, subsequently formed the first all-Negro band of note, one that played for three years at the Club Top Hat.

Cy McLean's band (it leaned in style to that of the great

Count Basie orchestra) was just one of many that contributed to the Canadian dance band scene. The sounds of the scene were many and varied because the Canadian bandleaders, like their American counterparts, offered a plethora of styles: Swing, dixieland, novelty and sweet.

And then there were the society bands, who, if they were versatile enough, and most of them were, combined a little bit of everything. Today, that little bit of everything signifies rock tunes and light rock arrangements, indicating that to survive you move with the times.

The society bands are still much in evidence, although their efforts are restricted to private parties rather than public events. Most famous of these were—and are—Stanley St. John, Frank Bogart, Bobby Gimby, Ellis McLintock, Johnny Lindon.

But again, with a nod to the times, many of the great events such as the debutante balls and huge house parties have disappeared. Today, the bands are more likely to be playing to big corporation dances but in essence the audiences are the same.

If the dancers are middle-aged their tastes usually run to Broadway tunes dating as far back as the twenties. They dance as well to the foxtrot, to waltzes and tangos, but they also like to swing and sway to Beatle tunes, to the Tijuana brass sounds and Latin American melodies.

Canadians still dance to their bands.

Helen McNamara

SECTION ONE

THE BANDS AND THE BALLROOMS

STANLEY ST. JOHN
AND HIS ORCHESTRA

The bands and the ballrooms. Somehow in Canada they went together. They did, too, in the United States but the Canadians, unlike their American colleagues, once they were established often remained for years in one dance spot.

In the United States it was a different system. The idea was to get booked into a ballroom, preferably a hotel ballroom, with a network radio outlet. The audience response was usually so enthusiastic that an orchestra could then move out on the road reaping the rewards of personal appearances, and sometimes movie contracts.

In the long run it was more profitable for the Canadian bands to stay put, and most of them did just that. The longer they stayed, the better known the ballroom became.

The time is long past since the Bert Niosi orchestra held forth for 18 consecutive years at the Palais Royale Ballroom yet there are dance fans who recall those times as the best of all times. In some cases it was the big bands (among them such historic names as Fletcher Henderson, Cab Calloway, Andy Kirk and Jimmy Lunceford along with the still thriving Duke Ellington, Count Basie and Woody Herman) that the crowds wanted to hear but many came away impressed with Niosi's 15 piece band. Not for nothing was he known as Canada's King of Swing.

Trump Davidson has enjoyed success from the day he organized his first band in 1936. Through the fifties and sixties his CBC radio broadcasts brought him a nation-wide audience. Yet there are fans who to this day think only of Trump Davidson in connection with the late, lamented Palace Pier.

When the Pier burned to the ground in January, 1963, it marked the end of a celebrated Canadian ballroom, a place of one night stands by the great U.S. name bands and the home of the Davidson band for 18 years.

It must be admitted that by the fifties the Pier had gone into a decline along with the big bands. The changing face of Toronto had nearly finished it. The old Pier, jutting out into Lake Ontario, close to where the Humber River flows into the lake, was rarely used. As Trump himself has remarked: "When they built the Gardiner Expressway you had to go almost to Oakville before you could turn around and get to the Pier."

Horace Lapp and orchestra at Banff Springs Hotel in 1939.

24

The Palais Royale, which started out as a restaurant in 1922, attracted thousands of dance band enthusiasts throughout the thirties and forties when Bert Niosi led the resident band and U.S. bands appeared on one-night stands.

CP Hotels

Most of Canada's leading dance bands have played in the Canadian Pacific's majestic Banff Springs Hotel in the Rocky Mountains in Banff, Alberta.

Along with the Pier many other ballrooms disappeared. Burned or demolished, turned into bingo palaces or skating arenas, the dance halls as Canadians knew them 30 or 40 years ago have vanished. Time has passed them by but Canadians who danced in them still grow nostalgic when the names of the ballrooms . . . and the bands who played in them . . . are brought to mind.

Here are a few . . .

THE ROMANELLIS

The Romanelli brothers have long since departed the Canadian dance band scene yet a romantic aura still hovers around the name . . . the Romanellis!

Luigi, Leo and Don were the best known but brothers Johnny and Joseph were also musicians, occasionally leading their own bands, sometimes sitting in with their brothers.

Their father, Joseph Romanelli was a well known harpist. Born in Italy, he had arrived in Canada when he was five and lived in Toronto until his death some 60 years later in 1944. His brother, Rocco Romanelli, a violinist, was equally acclaimed. Known as Romanelli the Great, he had as a young man accompanied Enrico Caruso and Madame Melba. On many visits to the U.S.A. Rocco conducted his own orchestra. He died in November, 1941, just a year before his famous nephew, Luigi, died suddenly, age 57, of a heart attack at the Manoir Richelieu where his band had played for four summers.

With the death of Luigi, the Canadian music world would never again be quite the same. Toronto musicians recall that there was a time in the thirties when the three bandleader brothers were working simultaneously in the city's leading supper clubs: Luigi at the King Edward Hotel's Oak Room; Don at the Royal York's Imperial Room and Leo at the Old Mill. Trump Davidson who played in Luigi's band from 1929 to 1936 says, "If you didn't work for the Romanellis you didn't work!"

1   The Romanellis in a picture taken in 1931. Luigi is in the imported sports car with U.S. bandleader Vincent Lopez at the steering wheel. Brother Leo looks on from the Cadillac.

2   Don Romanelli and his 13 man orchestra at the Royal York Hotel in 1931.

3   Don Romanelli and his orchestra on the Ontario lake ship, the Cayuga, around 1927.

4   Leo Romanelli and his orchestra

2

3

4

Luigi Romanelli and his orchestra at Manoir Richelieu, Murray Bay, Quebec, where they appeared for several summer seasons.

Luigi Romanelli's orchestra at the King Edward Hotel around 1923. Note the tuxedos and spats. Nat Cassels is the man in the reed department.

Luigi Romanelli's orchestra at the King Edward Hotel's Oak Room.

The Romanellis not only conducted their own hotel orchestras but sent out seven or eight bands under their name to various dance halls on Friday nights. Enrico DelGreco, a brother-in-law, often led these bands.

When Luigi died tributes arrived from musical organizations across Canada and the United States. With the help of radio broadcasts on the CBC and American networks he was by then internationally known. With the death of Don in 1960 and Leo in 1961, the Romanelli name disappeared from the country's musical ranks but wherever dance band musicians congregate it will never be forgotten.

In the twenties and through the thirties the Culleys were among Toronto's best known musicians, appearing in the city's ballrooms and theatres. Edwin, the youngest, recalls that his older brothers, Harry, Fred and George, and himself, the sons of Henry Teck Culley, a flautist with the Toronto Symphony Orchestra, were involved in most of the city's musical events.

Fred, who played violin, led his orchestra at the Royal York Hotel, the first Canadian band to play there when the hotel opened in June, 1929. Ben Bernie and his orchestra had been brought up from the United States to open the Imperial Room, a gala occasion when the cover charge was $10 per person. The Culley orchestra took over a few weeks later.

Previous to the Royal York opening Fred had been concert master with Fred Waring's Pennsylvanians, a band widely known for its slick instrumental and vocal arrangements. He wanted to take his own band into the states but the depression intervened. The Wickersham Commission appointed by President Hoover to enforce immigration laws, made it impossible for Canadian groups to cross the border. "So we disbanded," said Ed Culley. "Fred went back to Waring and Don Romanelli's orchestra went into the Royal York."

Fred, who had been musical director of Shea's Hippodrome in the early twenties, spent the rest of his life in the U.S.A. where he was Waring's musical director until he died in 1968. George, who played trumpet and had first appeared with Waring in 1921, died in 1948.

Harry, the oldest brother, and father of trombonist Ross Culley, now living in England, and Harry Culley, Jr., a saxophonist, was musical director of the Royal Alexandra Theatre for many years. Just before the war, he and his wife, Claudette, performed as a piano team, winning international attention when they toured England and South Africa with silent film stars Bebe Daniels and Ben Lyon. He died in 1970.

Another noted member of the family is William R. Culley, who played trombone in theatre orchestras, until he joined the Toronto Symphony in 1940 and stayed there until 1955. He is a nephew of Teck Culley who died in 1948.

Saxophonist Ed Culley was a member of the original Glen Gray orchestra when it appeared at Casa Loma in 1927. He might have become a permanent member of the Waring organization but in 1934 when he travelled to Cleveland for a hotel opening, he was unable to continue to New York with Waring. "As a travelling musician I wasn't allowed to stay," he said. Instead he returned to Toronto and resumed his career as a dance band musician, a career that had begun with Gilbert Watson's band in the twenties.

HORACE LAPP

When Horace Lapp was accompanist to commentator Kate Aitken on her nationally known broadcast he noticed one day that the lady's script was going up in flames. "Mrs. A. liked to smoke," said Horace, "and this day she had accidentally dropped her lit match on her script." A slight panic ensued. "Cy Strange, our announcer, didn't know what was going to happen next. The engineer ran in carrying a bottle of seltzer water. Me? I was playing There'll Be A Hot Time in the Old Town Tonight."

Somehow that story tells more about Horace Lapp than a full length biography. Wherever his career took him, Horace viewed the world with an irrepressible humour. Even today, his age hovering around a vigorous 70 years, he continues to delight audiences. Lapp provides piano accompaniment for silent movies at half a dozen locations in and around Toronto, including the Ontario Science Centre.

It's an assignment he does to perfection. At the very beginning of his career in the twenties Horace played piano and organ with Jack Arthur's Orchestra at Shea's Hippodrome, Imperial and Uptown theatres. Alone or with the orchestra he learned to improvise music for the films.

Theatre work was also part of his job when he joined Luigi Romanelli's orchestra. "I worked for Luigi when he was musical director at the Allen Theatre which later became the Tivoli. We'd play the afternoon show, then go on to the King Edward Hotel to play the dinner dance with Luigi's trio."

When Horace organized his first orchestra, which opened at the Royal Muskoka Hotel in 1934, then moved on to the Royal York Hotel in 1936, his band was a little different from all others.

The first thing he did was have his men learn to tap dance. "I was all showbusiness," he says. "We'd announce 'Ladies and gentlemen, the floor show!' and the musicians would get out on the floor and dance. It was terrible!"

Musically, the 14 piece orchestra was first rate including at various times such noted musicians as flautist Gordon Day (his mother was sister of Teck Culley), Trump Davidson, Cliff McKay, Moe Koffman, Bobby Gimby and Bill McCauley who was to become the O'Keefe Centre's musical director in the sixties.

Lapp's fine theatrical touch even extended to the band's ap-

Fred Culley with one of Toronto's
first dance bands. His brother, Ed
Culley, is next to him, seated, in
saxophone section.

Horace Lapp at the piano with
the orchestra he conducted at the Royal York Hotel from 1936 to 1945.

Horace Lapp and his first orchestra at the Royal Muskoka Hotel in 1934. The guitarist is Ted Andrews, step-father of actress-singer Julie Andrews.

pearance. Before intermission the men came out wearing white suits. After intermission they re-appeared in red jackets. Some evenings they wore tails. But it was worth the effort. The average size crowd was 700 to 800 dancers nightly, with a minimum of 1,000 on Friday and Saturday evenings.

The Horace Lapp Orchestra played close to nine years in the Royal York, and never, says Horace, "ran into the red." Among the best years were the war years "when the place went mad, filled with soldiers and airmen out for a good time. They were a marvellous audience."

"Yes," he said. "After I went to the CBC I made a lot of money but it was never quite as much fun." Except, of course, that day when he gave his own hot version of There'll Be A Hot Time In the Old Town Tonight.

BERT NIOSI

Bert Niosi, a native of London, Ontario, and the member of another musical family (his brother Joe plays bass; his younger brother, the late Johnny Niosi, played drums) could easily have followed in the footsteps of fellow Londoner, Guy Lombardo. He did, in fact, play in one of Lombardo's first bands in the U.S.A. but Bert never had any great desire to leave Canada.

One of the most versatile musicians in the country, proficient on clarinet, flute, saxophone, trumpet and trombone, he had received offers from many American leaders including Jimmy Dorsey, Gene Krupa and Glen Gray but he had seen enough of the travelling life to turn them down.

In his youth a student of Professor Pasquale Venuta, the same man who had taught Guy, Carmen and Lebert Lombardo, Bert was playing professionally at 12 years in a Chinese cafe and on the road with the Lombardos at 14. At 19 Bert formed his own band and played for summer resort crowds at Port Stanley until 1931 when he took a nine piece band into Toronto's Embassy Club. A year later he opened at the Palais Royale where he conducted the band until 1950.

By the fifties, Bert was working in the CBC's Toronto studios as composer, arranger and conductor. Seven of those years he was also a performer appearing on the Happy Gang radio show, along with brother Joe. The two of them later collaborated on the aptly titled song, My Brother and I.

The band was gone but the memories lingered on. In the summer of 1972, the Bert Niosi band was brought back to the Palais for a one-night stand. The crowd was smaller than it used to be (1,000 instead of the 2,000 that usually arrived at the Palais in the forties) but the middle-age jitterbugs cheered the leader and his men with all the vigour of their youth.

TRUMP DAVIDSON

Like so many Canadian musicians, Trump Davidson, or Jimmy as he is known to family and friends, was a Romanelli alumnus. Fresh from his home town of Sudbury in northern Ontario, Trump had joined Luigi's orchestra in 1929. He was hired as a singer, but eventually, as he had hoped, played trumpet in the band. The association with Romanelli lasted seven years. In 1936 he took his own band into a night club called Club Esquire, later re-named the Club Top Hat.

A few months later Ray Noble, the British bandleader, discovered the Davidson band when he was in Toronto, leading a notable band of his own, at Shea's Hippodrome Theatre. In the personnel were no less than Glenn Miller, Claude Thornhill, Charlie Spivak and Bud Freeman.

It was a compliment then to Trump that Noble had chosen the Canadian band for his British tour. Among the Davidson men were musicians slated to win recognition on their own. One of them was Johnny Burt, who in the early forties was to spend two years as arranger for Paul Whiteman.

Davidson and his men spent 1937 and 1938 touring the British Isles, returning home in 1939 when war appeared imminent. A year later Trump took his band into the Dardanella Ballroom at Wasaga Beach, then to Hull, Quebec, for four months. When

Trump Davidson and his band, around 1936, just before they sailed to England to begin a two year tour with British bandleader Ray Noble. Among members of the orchestra were Joe Niosi, Jack Madden, Vern Kahanen, Cokie Campbell, Ted Davidson, Johnny Burt and Reef McGarvey.

Trump Davidson, one of the country's top bandleaders, with the band he led at the Palace Pier for 18 years.

he returned he joined Horace Lapp's orchestra at the Royal York as a sideman. In 1944 he formed his own band, opened at the Palace Pier and stayed for 18 years, until the Pier was burned down in 1963.

Among the men who have been featured with his band through the years are Harvey Silver, piano; brother Ted David-son, tenor saxophone; Reef McGarvey, drums; Murray Ginsberg, trombone; Cliff McKay, clarinetist and TV-radio star.

MART KENNEY

While most Canadian dance bands became identified with one or two cities, Mart Kenney and His Western Gentlemen belonged to the whole country.

That seven man group was organized in 1931 and made its debut at the Alexandra Ballroom in Vancouver. From there it became a roving band, barnstorming through rural British Columbia,

Mart Kenney and the original Western Gentlemen.

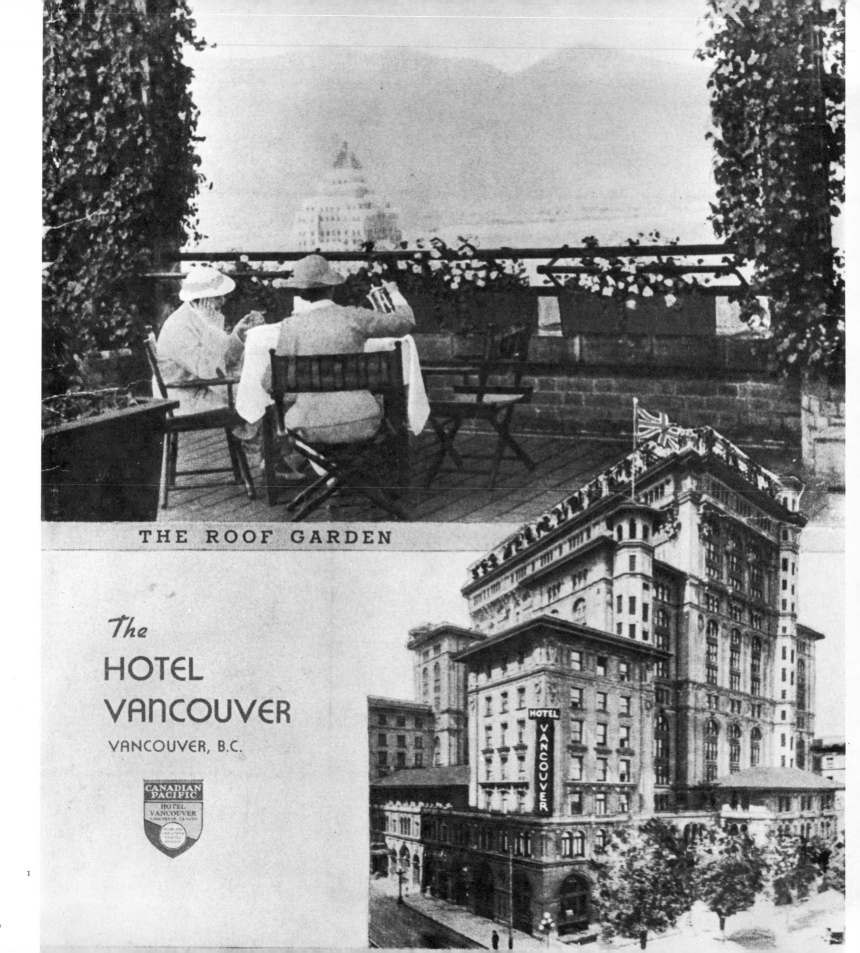

THE ROOF GARDEN

The
HOTEL
VANCOUVER
VANCOUVER, B.C.

CANADIAN PACIFIC
HOTEL
VANCOUVER

38

going off on a theatre tour, playing a series of dates that took the band into the Alberta Rockies, to the Hotel Saskatchewan in Regina, to the Banff Springs Hotel, to Chateau Lake Louise and the Hotel Vancouver.

Its personnel included Art Hallman, who became a noted bandleader in his own right. His colleagues were Jack Hemmings, trumpet; Glen Griffiths, trumpet, accordion and piano; Bert Lister,

1 *The Hotel Vancouver where many Canadian dance bands appeared over the years.*

2 *The Mart Kenney orchestra at the Spanish Grill in the Hotel Vancouver.*

3 *The Rocky Mountains provide an appropriate backdrop for Mart Kenney's orchestra, most famous of all the western bands. In the personnel are Art Hallman (on Kenney's right) and Stan Patton (second from right) who later led their own bands.*

tenor sax, baritone sax and guitar; Ed Emel, drummer, and Hec MacCallum, bass, who eventually went into the talent booking business in Toronto.

In 1934, the band's theme, The West, A Nest And You, Dear, became a favourite of Canadians when the Kenney aggregation was presented on the Canadian Radio Broadcasting Commission network, forerunner of the CBC. In 1938, the Kenney men made their first recordings for RCA Victor, continuing to turn out their hits on that label for several years.

In Art Hallman's words: "The Mart Kenney band was *the* band." During the war it was permanently established as Canada's leading dance orchestra when, under the auspices of the Coca Cola Company of Canada it toured army camps and war plants, and presented a series of half hour broadcasts known as the Victory Parade on the CBC English and French networks. Says Hallman: "We went across Canada 14 times in three years."

Kenney had first played at the Royal York Hotel in the late thirties, then returned for a three year run in 1946. In 1949 Mart introduced a bit of the west to the east when he opened his own Mart Kenney Ranch, a hall that accommodated over 1,000 dancers in Woodbridge, Ont., near Toronto. For six months of the year

Mart and his band and his wife, vocalist Norma Locke, who had joined the orchestra in the forties, appeared there on weekends, six months of the year, spending the remainder of each year touring the west.

Today, the Kenneys are back in the west, living in Mission City, B.C. Norma rarely sings now, but Kenney still plays occasional dates. The rest of the time he sells real estate and enjoys it. In or out of the music world, his name is still prominent. He's president of the Chamber of Commerce and chairman of publicity for the Easter Seal campaign in British Columbia.

Dal Richards' Hotel Vancouver Orchestra at the Panorama Roof in 1960. Lorraine McAllister, his wife, was vocalist with the band which included saxophonist Lance Harrison, nationally known dixieland jazz band leader.

DAL RICHARDS

Dal Richards, widely known as Mr. Music, led a celebrated band on the west coast. For 26 years the Richards orchestra was based at the Panorama Roof of the Hotel Vancouver playing at many other functions as well. But wherever the band played, it was invariably introduced as Dal Richards and His Hotel Vancouver Orchestra — The Band At The Top of The Town.

Other places on the agenda included the Empress Hotel in Victoria, the Olympic Hotel in Seattle and the Jantzen Beach Ballroom in Portland, Oregon. In the U.S. the band was heard regularly on the CBS network. In Canada, it broadcast over the CBC's two networks and during the war provided a round-the-world transcription service to Canadian servicemen.

Richards led his band from April, 1940, to August, 1966, which could be the longest period any Canadian dance band has played in one ballroom. It was a rewarding experience he finds. "If there is one fact that emerges more than any other in looking back

Dal Richards — Surrounded!

at that long stay at the roof it is the number of people who tell me that they remember the night they were at the roof on their engagement, or anniversary, or a special birthday or before leaving for overseas. Even now in my various travels I frequently meet people who pass such a comment. It's rather gratifying, as a matter of fact."

With Richards through the years were a number of well-known vocalists including Juliette, who sang with the band from 1940 to 1943, Beryl Boden, Judy Richards, Terry Dale, Elan Stuart and Lorraine McAllister who became his wife.

Since he left the Panorama Roof, Richards has moved into the hotel management field, presently working at the Jet Inn at the Sea-Tac International Airport in Seattle, Washington. However, he's still active musically, conducting a big band for such events as the annual Variety Club Telethon, the annual Automobile Show, acting as musical director of the Pacific Coliseum Startime Shows and the Half Time shows for the B.C. Lions. As he says: "There is still lots of music for me."

Stan Patton with the orchestra he led at the Spanish Grill. When Patton gave up the band in 1939 it was taken over by Dal Richards.

STAN PATTON

Stan Patton, who was born in Vancouver, organized his first band in 1934 and spent the ensuing five years at the Alma Academy, the Casino, the Hotel Vancouver's Spanish Grill and the Alexandra Ballroom in Vancouver. In 1939, Patton gave up the band which was taken over by Dal Richards at the Hotel Vancouver's Panorama Roof. A year later Stan joined Mart Kenney's orchestra which came east to play an engagement at the Brant Inn, Burlington, Ont. and to appear on the Purity Flour radio show in Toronto. In 1941, once more heading his own band, Stan appeared at the Brant Inn, the Gatineau Country Club, Casa Loma and the Royal York Hotel. Three years later Patton again disbanded when he found it increasingly difficult to find good musicians during the war years and began working as a free lance arranger in eastern Canada. When Patton, in late 1945, again organized a band, this time an all-reed orchestra, it was acclaimed by his many fans.

Stan Patton and his orchestra on the roof of the Hotel Vancouver.

MOXIE WHITNEY

Moxie Whitney enjoyed one of the longest house band engagements in Canadian dance band history. In 1948, that personable gentleman (his first name is actually Moxam) took his orchestra into the Royal York's Imperial Room and stayed until 1971. In the intervening years he had helped build the room into a nationally known big-name night club. At the same time he booked talent for other Canadian Pacific hotels in Canada.

His departure had been triggered by management's change of policy but Whitney felt that he was due for a change himself. Only once during the previous 23 years had he played elsewhere. That was when the hotel staff went on strike in 1962 and Moxie took his band off to Honolulu and a year's engagement at the Royal Hawaiian Hotel.

Moxie Whitney and his orchestra at the Royal York Hotel where he appeared from 1948 to 1971.

Moxie, who has seven children, now resides in the Grand Cayman Island in the British West Indies where he owns the Royal Palms Hotel. From that "paradise island" Whitney maintains contact with his Toronto office where Whitney orchestras are booked for engagements around the city.

His history as a dance band leader goes back to the age of 17 when he made his debut leading a quartet at Weston Town Hall. His first big break came in 1937 when his band, then known as

the Pacific Swingsters played at Riley's Pavilion near Trenton. During the war, with the RCAF he played trumpet in an air force band and recalls that he "was the first and only steel guitarist to play with the RCAF Central band in Rockcliffe."

During the early forties while working with Stanley St. John's band at the CNE, Moxie met most of the name band leaders and sidemen of the time. "This gave me an insight into the band business which I might never have had," says Moxie. "I met and got to know Charlie Christian, Lionel Hampton, Bud Freeman, Alvino Rey and many others."

From the beginning of his Imperial Room engagement Moxie had always insisted upon music for a dancing public; from the first night in 1948 when there were only 11 people in the room, of which, he says with a laugh, "five were relatives."

By the sixties such name acts as Ella Fitzgerald, Peggy Lee, Duke Ellington, Count Basie and Guy Lombardo were attracting capacity audiences. Whitney was signing acts that could ask for $15,000 or more. The cover charge in some cases went up to $8 per person, a far cry from the early forties when the admission price was $2.

A strong believer in giving the public what it wants, Whitney says that in the forties he catered strictly to a dancing public. "Entertainment was rare, unless the boys in the band put on funny hats and marched around the room. We did that, too. We were the show as well as being the dance band."

CY McLEAN

Cy McLean, back in the forties, formed the first all-Negro dance band of note in Canada. There had been other bands but it was Cy's that caught the public fancy. In late 1944 Cy opened at the Club Top Hat, alternating with other orchestras, for the next three years. Prior to the Top Hat, McLean led a band, originally formed by trumpeter Roy Worrell, at Fallingbrook Pavilion (dubbed the East Enders' Paradise) located at the foot of 100 steps leading down to Lake Ontario. (Another home of happy feet for east end Torontonians was the nearby Balmy Beach Club.)

Cy, a native of Sydney, Nova Scotia, arrived in Toronto in the thirties, at the age of 16. Back home he had studied violin, then switched to piano. His reputation as a talented musician was soon discovered. When he was 12 years old, Sax Hector and His Jubilee Singers came up from Boston to do a concert. "Sax wanted a coloured pianist and he heard that I could play," Cy recalls. "So he spoke to my dad and persuaded him to let me do the concert. That night one of the big numbers was Tiger Rag and Sax yelled at me to take a solo. I put my best foot forward."

Cy McLean has been doing that ever since. Now the leader of a trio (with Gordon Phillips on guitar and Tommy Oakie playing drums) he has acquired a reputation as one of the finest jazz pianists in Canada. Ask Earl Hines. When that world famous pianist, was appearing at the Colonial Tavern he had to fly back to New York for a TV date. The man he chose to take his place was Cy McLean.

FRANK BOGART

One September evening in 1967, a singular honour was paid Frank Bogart, one of Canada's leading society band leaders. That night someone else was leading his band and Bogart couldn't have been happier.

Bogart and his orchestra were celebrating their 25th anniversary with the Granite Club. On hand to mark the occasion and to lead the band was Lester Lanin, one of the undisputed leaders of American society bands.

The two had been friends for years which is hardly surprising. Like Lanin, Bogart had built up a fantastic following with several of his orchestras continually in demand by wealthy socialites. Besides the Granite Club, Bogart's orchestras had played at the Royal Canadian Yacht Club, at country clubs, annual balls, house parties and weddings.

Born in Woodstock, Ont., Frank had attended school in Hamilton and at 18 had joined Ferde Mowry's band. Five years later he was leading his own band at the Brant Inn in Burlington, Ont., then for three years led an orchestra that included Gordon Delamont, Benny Winestone, Teddy Roderman and the late Jack Kane at the Club Top Hat.

With his present bands, Bogart can send out a group anywhere from three to 15 men, capable of playing everything from "danceable" rock and jazz to big band music. Even so, it's a tough age for dance orchestras. A large party can cover an age span of 17 to 60 years and every age group wants its own kind of music. "The older people ask us to play their music and then the young people say 'cut out that mom and dad music!'," says Bogart.

ELLIS McLINTOCK

Ellis McLintock celebrated his 20th anniversary as a dance band leader appropriately at Casa Loma. It was there that his orchestra played its first engagement on June 2, 1944.

One of Canada's most accomplished musicians, McLintock won acclaim for his trumpet playing in Canada, England and the United States before he was 20. A student of his father, Ellis, Sr., a brass instrumentalist, he learned to play trumpet at eight years. At 14 he appeared with the British Empire Boys' Band in London, England; a year later he won the Open Canadian Championship for trumpet. At 17 he was principal trumpeter of the Toronto

Philharmonic Orchestra and the Toronto Symphony Orchestra. At 19 he was invited to join the All-American Youth Orchestra, conducted by Leopold Stokowski and toured North America with this group in 1941. When he returned to Canada, he joined the RCAF and as might be expected his talent as a musician was soon put to use as trumpet soloist with the RCAF Central Band in Ottawa.

When his stint with the RCAF ended, Ellis resumed his career in Toronto where he continued to play with the Toronto Symphony, to conduct his dance orchestra and to appear on CBC radio and TV programs.

Cy McLean led a band at the Club Top Hat for three years starting around 1945.

Pianist leader Frank Bogart playing his first job at the Brant Inn, Burlington, Ont. in 1940.

Benny Louis and his orchestra in a 1952 photo at Casa Loma. Band members included Norman Symonds, Bernie Piltch, Herb Spanier and Fred Stone. The vocalist is Anne Gable, who later sang in the U.S.A.

Ellis McLintock and his orchestra at Casa Loma where he began his career as a dance band leader in 1944. At the piano is Benny Louis who became a leader himself.

Still a leader, McLintock has made several recordings for the Canadian Talent Library, but perhaps his best known recording, particularly among dance band fans, is an LP featuring him at still another well known dance spot. It's his first RCA Victor album: Ellis McLintock at the Old Mill.

The Old Mill, where Ellis appeared from 1960 to 1968, was one of many ballrooms where he has performed since his Casa Loma debut. Through the years he has led his orchestra at the Palais Royale, the Palace Pier, Bigwin Inn, Brant Inn and Belmont Park in Montreal.

BENNY LOUIS

Until Benny Louis formed his own band in 1946, he played piano with several Toronto orchestras, including those of Don Romanelli, Ellis McLintock and Bobby Gimby. At the same time he was writing arrangements for radio shows.

Born in Niagara Falls, he moved to Toronto in 1939 where he started taking orchestration lessons. In the late forties he resumed his studies, this time with the noted Canadian composer John Weinzweig. Shortly after he formed his band he appeared on several occasions at Montreal's Belmont Park.

Louis' band, often featured at the city's leading social events, proved to be a showcase of stars. In its ranks at one time or another were vocalists Margo McKinnon, who went on to television; Dianne Stapley, who became a revue singer-actress; Penny Machtel, later a cabaret singer, and Anne Marie Moss, who with her husband, Jackie Paris, now sings in U.S. night clubs. Musicians who came out of the Benny Louis band were Moe Koffman, who will be forever known for his Swinging Shepherd Blues and his jazz prowess on flute and saxophones; Marshall Olchowy, an alto saxophone player who won the Michigan State jazz soloist contest in 1968; Fred Stone, who played trumpet with Duke Ellington's orchestra in the sixties; alto saxist Norman Symonds, now an internationally known composer.

Louis still leads a band in Toronto, but the style has changed considerably. Today, he favours contemporary rock.

BOBBY GIMBY

To most Canadians Bobby Gimby is the Pied Piper of Canada. The sensation created by his song, Ca-na-da in 1967, made the Saskatchewan-born composer-arranger-leader known from coast to coast.

The Gimby name is actually known much farther afield. In 1961, while on a world tour with his wife and daughter Gimby visited a Singapore convent where he heard a group of youngsters singing. He was so enthused by their enthusiasm that he wrote them a song, Malaysia Forever, that so delighted the inhabitants that it was accepted as a popular anthem. Malaysia Radio began to call him The Pied Piper From Canada.

When Bobby wrote Ca-na-da it was only logical that he be

Bobby Gimby and his orchestra celebrate the Yuletide season in 1950 at Mart Kenney's ranch in Woodbridge, Ont. Among the members of the band: Eddie Karam, Rudy Toth, Erich Traugott, Doug Pierce and Jack Sweetman.

Still the same place, the same date but the wives and sweethearts of the Gimby musicians have taken over. That's Bobby's daughter, little Lynne Gimby in the front row getting ready to play clarinet.

dubbed The Pied Piper of Canada. Since Centennial year, recordings of Ca-na-da have soared past 400,000 (comparable to a few million in U.S. terms) and it's now estimated that there are 50 commercial recordings. At least 250 school choirs and bands have recorded the song. In 1971 Gimby presented the original manuscript and all future royalties to the Boy Scouts of Canada.

Now in demand for school functions across the land, the indefatigable Gimby also has five dance bands operating under his name in Toronto. His career as a dance band musician began with Mart Kenney's orchestra as lead trumpeter and soloist in Vancouver. Eventually he moved to Toronto where his first orchestra made its debut at the Brant Inn in the mid-forties. A couple years later he joined the CBC's Happy Gang, staying with the show until its end in 1959.

PAT RICCIO

Pat Riccio, winner of the best dance band in Ontario contest in 1960, is a leader whose experience dates back to war years. In 1941 Riccio joined the RCAF, soon after becoming arranger and musical director of the RCAF Streamliners, a band that the late Glenn Miller praised as one of the finest dance bands he had ever heard. Miller had ample opportunity to hear the Canadian band because his own famous orchestra alternated with it during an engagement at the Queensbury Club in London, England, in 1944.

After the war Riccio returned to Toronto where he played clarinet and saxophones in the orchestras of Bert Niosi, Maynard Ferguson, Art Hallman and Mart Kenney. In 1947 he won top honours as Canada's best alto saxophonist. In 1957 Riccio's own band made its debut at Oshawa's Jubilee Pavilion, three years later winning top place in the 1960 contest.

Drummer Don Hilton, Paul Grosney on trumpet, and Pat Riccio, saxophone (he led the RCAF Streamliners) in wartime London, England.

FERDE MOWRY

Ferde Mowry, whose name was synonymous with the Club Embassy where he was a big name in the thirties, got his start as a dance band leader while still in high school. Along with several students at a Peterboro, Ontario, high school Mowry formed a co-operative band that played in nearby resorts until it opened at Toronto's Embassy in 1932. When the club closed in the summer months, the Mowry men played to vacationers at Port Elgin and Southampton. Out of that band in later years came two leaders: pianist Frank Bogart, who leads one of the best known society orchestras in Canada, and the late Gordon Braund, who eventually played trumpet with Mart Kenney and Moxie Whitney's orchestras and later led his own band at the Old Mill.

A popular band in the thirties was the Ferde Mowry Orchestra at the Embassy in Toronto. Among its members was Gordon Braund, who eventually returned to the Embassy leading his own band. Trumpeter Braund also played in the Mart Kenney and Moxie Whitney orchestras.

Ferde Mowry and his orchestra at the Embassy Club in 1941.

and not to be forgotten

...IN THE TWENTIES

Capt. Plunkett's Dumbells included some well known musicians in the early twenties. Among them were Morris London on trumpet and Nat Cassels, second saxophonist from right.

Jack Evans and His Manhattan Blue Blowers, circa 1924.

Billy Bissett, another early Toronto bandleader, with his orchestra at the Silver Slipper. Bissett was later known as Billy Bishop in the U.S.A.

...IN THE THIRTIES

Jack Slatter and his band, popular in the thirties.

Joe DeCourcy and His Orchestra played in many Ontario ballrooms, notably the Chateau Laurier in Ottawa, the Connaught Hotel in Hamilton and the Old Mill in Toronto. A noted member of the band was clarinetist Cliff McKay who later became a CBC-TV star.

Nelson Hatch with the band he took into the Old Mill after it was renovated in the thirties.

Ozzie Williams, who began leading a band in 1932, played for several years at Toronto's Club Kingsway. A comedy routine was part of the program.

Harry Bedlington and His Whispering Orchestra when they appeared at Toronto's Savarin in the thirties.

Gene Fogerty and his Toronto band of the thirties.

Jack Denny with the three pianos he featured at the Mount Royal Hotel in Montreal.

Stan Williams orchestra at Robertson's Ballroom in Hamilton, Ont. Harry Houston is the drummer.

George Sims and his orchestra at Lakefield, Ontario, the summer of 1932. Trombonist Murray McEachern (second from right) joined Benny Goodman's orchestra four years later.

George Hooey with the band he led at the Beaches Masonic Hall in Toronto's east end in the late thirties.

Bus Browne and Boys, a band of the thirties, included the celebrated Canadian composer, Robert Farnon, who now lives in England. Farnon is second from right, next to Homer Watson who later led the Modernaires. George Hooey is fourth from left.

Earl Melloway poses with his Montreal orchestra at the Venetian Gardens. Nat Cassels, who soon after formed his own band, is the first saxophonist.

Jack Barry and His Orchestra at Belmont Manor, in Bermuda.

A 1934 photo of the Larry Fagan orchestra at Clear Lake, Manitoba.

The noted Brown Brothers, conducted by Roy Brown, formed the nucleus of a well known band in the west. The orchestra appeared at Clear Lake, Manitoba, in the summer months; at Brandon's Esquire Ballroom in the winter.

Charles Dornberger and his orchestra in a 1938 photo. This was an American band that played in Canada for about five years.

CHARLES DORNBERGER
and his Mount Royal Hotel Orchestra

Gordon Day and His Rhythm Knights, one of Toronto's early dance bands.

...IN THE FORTIES

Eddie Stroud's orchestra as it appeared at the Barclay Hotel in the forties. The band also spent several years at the Savarin and during summer months at Dunn's Pavilion in Bala, Ont. The personnel included the leader's brothers, drummer George Stroud and first saxophonist Ron Stroud. The vocalist is Babs Babineau later noted for her work in the commercial music field.

Denny Vaughan, singing at the microphone, with the Stan Patton band at the Brant Inn in Burlington, Ont.

Wally Koster, who was to become nationally known for his singing on CBC programs, is the man taking the trombone solo in this photo of Herbie Brittain's band at Winnipeg Auditorium in 1941.

Don Wright's orchestra at Grand Beach, Manitoba, in 1942. Paul Grosney, who later became a bandleader in Winnipeg and Toronto, is second from right in back row.

Monty Levine's band played at the Flame Cabaret in Winnipeg in 1945-46.

Gordon Delamont with his b[...] at the Club Top Hat in 1947. Tru[...] peter Delamont (standing at left[...] today an internationally known tea[...] er of arranging and composing.

The Modernaires, a co-operative band that flourished in the forties, often appeared at the Sea Breeze, the Beaches and West End Masonic Halls in Toronto, at the Wonderland in London, Ont., and the Winnipeg Auditorium. In 1941-2 the band was chosen to play opposite the big bands in the CNE tent. Trombonist Homer Watson was the leader; Mary Bates, the singer.

MASONIC TEMPLE
YONGE ST. AT DAVENPORT

PAUL FIRMAN'S GREAT BAND

ROOF GARDEN
HANLAN'S POINT

Paul Firman's popular band, seen here at the Masonic Temple in 1944, included several well-known sidemen. Joe Niosi was on bass. Two future leaders were pianist Bill Isbister and saxophonist Doug Kemp. In the trumpet section, extreme right is Jimmy Reynolds, who was acclaimed that year by Band Leaders magazine as "the most successful sideman in Canada."

Morgan Thomas with his band at Crystal Beach, 1941-42.

1   *Jimmy Namaro with his big band of the forties.*

2   *Norman Harris' band performs at Kenwick-On-The-Lake, Sarnia, in 1948. Dunc Snider is the drummer. Standing in second row, second from left, is saxophonist, Harry Culley.*

3   *Stanley St. John at the piano, led a society band for years in Toronto. The young guitarist, at right, is Moxie Whitney.*

4   *Stanley St. John and his first band.*

...IN THE FIFTIES

Doug Kemp with his ba[...] Masonic Auditorium in down[...] Toronto where he appeared thr[...] out the fifties.

Art Hallman and his or[...] tra, back of the Uptown Theatr[...] the early fifties. That trombo[...] looks familiar? Yes, it's come[...] Jerry Colonna.

Ron Wicken's orchestra at the Alexandra Ballroom in Hamilton, Ontario, circa 1950.

Wally (left) and Ron Wicken, who grew up in Galt, Ontario, each enjoyed successful musical careers. Ron, popularly known as "Darkie" Wicken, played drums in dance bands for over 50 years. In 1938, billed as Canada's premier drummer, he organized his first band but disbanded when war was declared. Following a two year stint with the RCAF, he joined Mart Kenney's Western Gentlemen. In 1947 he took his own band into Hamilton's Alexandra Ballroom for a short engagement and stayed 13 years. Meanwhile, brother Wally Wicken was leading his own band at the Club Norman, Toronto's first night club. In 1951, he began leading a trio at the Embassy Hotel where he played non-stop for the next 11 years.

Pianist Jan August accompanied by trumpeter Paul Grosney's orchestra at Winnipeg's Roseland Ballroom in 1950.

Jack Denton's orchestra played at most of Toronto's dance band clubs through the fifties and sixties. Among them were the Palais Royale, Club Top Hat, Casa Loma, the Old Mill, the Palace Pier, where this photo was taken, and Oshawa's Jubilee Pavilion.

Johnny Lindon and his society orchestra widely known for its appearances at conventions, weddings and social events in Toronto. The Lindon band, seen here with June Sheath (left) and his sister, Louise Lindon, with the leader at the extreme right, played ten consecutive seasons at the Royal York's Imperial Room.

Boyd Valleau and his orchestra
at the Jubilee Pavilion in Oshawa,
Ont. in 1944.

Art Hallman (left) with Joan Fairfax, who went on to lead her own band in the sixties. With them are sidemen Johnny Cowell, now a member of the Toronto Symphony and a prolific songwriter, and Harry Hamilton, who is now a school music teacher. Both men played trumpet in the Hallman orchestra.

Every Canadian dance band had its singer; sometimes male, but more often female. The singer added a touch of glamour to the band stand. That was something dance band fans appreciated even if some of the singers would have been better off warbling in the shower.

Nevertheless, many Canadian band vocalists went on to successful solo careers and almost everyone of them looks upon the dance band phase of their careers as invaluable experience. As Lorraine McAllister, for years featured vocalist with husband Dal Richards' band in Vancouver, says: "The best possible preparation for a popular singing career is to sing with the dance bands."

Here are some who started their careers just that way . . .

ART HALLMAN

Art Hallman has led a band of his own since the forties and he's still active but his role in the Canadian dance band scene is actually two fold.

Not only is he a well known band leader but he has contributed greatly to the vocal scene as a singer himself and as the coach of several singers who went on to individual fame.

If singing plays an important part in his musical career it's easy to understand. Even as a youngster he was singing in school choirs and headed for an operatic career until, that is, the day he discovered popular music. From then on he divided his time between singing and playing the saxophone and piano.

At 19 Hallman took a job in a hardware company (that was in his native Vancouver) but he was so engrossed in his music that he quit his job and spent the summer with a ship's orchestra. "That summer I made 14 round trips to Alaska," he recalls, "then I joined CJOR in Vancouver as staff pianist."

It was a lucky move for the young musician. "The station was above the Alexandra Ballroom where Mart Kenney's band played. Mart wanted a singer who could also play piano and made me an offer. That's how I became the seventh Western Gentleman in the Kenney orchestra."

Hallman stayed with Kenney for 13 years then decided it was time to go out on his own. With his band, a 15 piece outfit that opened at Casa Loma in 1945, Art sang a lot but he also featured other vocalists, always female, who gave the band a romantic charm audiences adored.

Hallman, so time has proven, had an unerring ability to choose attractive girls headed for stardom. For one, there was Shirley Harmer, the little girl from Thornton's Corners near Oshawa, Ontario, who eventually had her own show and is now an internationally known night club singer.

Blonde Joan Fairfax, an exceedingly gifted girl, who now writes her own arrangements and for a time led her own band, sang with Hallman as well as Marilyn Kent, who was chosen Miss Canada of 1952; Terry Dale, now the wife of broadcaster Alan

Millar, who was featured for several years on the Wayne and Shuster shows, and Lorraine McAllister.

The girls who sang in the Hallman band were fortunate because Hallman, a noted vocal coach in the fifties, helped them overcome singing problems. "I took advanced people only," said Art. "They were usually singers who had problems perhaps in intonation or phrasing or perhaps the quality of their voices needed changing." For example, Hallman remembers that he helped Joan Fairfax bring her semi-legit soprano voice into a contralto range.

Still one of the country's busiest bandleaders, Hallman has since given up female vocalists. "I dropped all the girl singers eventually," he said rather ruefully. "They all got married."

JOAN FAIRFAX

Joan Fairfax, who for several years enjoyed top billing on CBC-TV shows, now lives in Coral Springs, Florida. Early in the fifties, Joan spent a year singing with Art Hallman's orchestra and a season with Frank Bogart's band. It was Hallman who suggested that she change from her concert style of singing to popular music which proved to be valuable advice. Throughout the fifties she appeared on Music Hall, the Denny Vaughan show, the Wayne and Shuster Hour and then starred on her own show, with an all-girl orchestra, in 1959-60. In 1961 she moved to the United States where she appeared several times on the Jack Paar show, with Ed Sullivan and Lawrence Welk. In 1964 she made headlines as the leader of an all-girl orchestra that, on the recommendation of Guy Lombardo, was booked into the Roosevelt Grill and received rave notices. Joan has since broken up the band because as she puts it, "Girls aren't good travellers. They don't like to be away from home all the time." Nevertheless Joan still travels, appearing at conventions all over the U.S.A. and still continues to write her own arrangements, a skill she learned as a student of the noted Toronto teacher, Gordon Delamont.

LORRAINE McALLISTER

Lorraine McAllister, star of several CBC programs not only sang with the bands, but married one of the west coast's best known bandleaders. The wife of Dal Richards, she sang with his band at the Hotel Vancouver for several years, following appearances with the Kenney Peaker Orchestra in Saskatoon, the Montreal bands of Johnny Holmes and Maynard Ferguson, Art Hallman's orchestra at the Brant Inn, Casa Loma and the Royal York Hotel and Moxie Whitney's band at the Royal York. As a member of the Lester Cole Debutante Singing Group she spent a year in the U.S.A. in the early fifties, then returned to Canada where she appeared on a succession of CBC radio and television shows, including Cross Canada Hit Parade, Cliff McKay's Holiday Ranch and her own shows, Meet Lorraine and Lorraine Sings.

NORMA LOCKE

Norma Locke can quite likely claim the longest singing engagement with one band. For 25 years she sang with Mart Kenney's orchestra from the time she joined the band in 1944, marrying the leader in 1952, right up until Kenney went into semi-retirement in 1969. Today, the famous musical couple live in Mission City, B.C.

Born in Ottawa, Norma came to Toronto when she was 18 to study voice at the Royal Conservatory of Music. Later she helped pay her tuition singing with Joe DeCourcy's band at the Old Mill, then with Howard Cable's band at Dunn's Pavilion in Bala, Ont. Besides her singing, Norma also writes songs. She studied composition first with Godfrey Ridout, producing some popular songs in the late fifties including When I Get Back To Calgary and Christmas Is a-Comin'. In the early sixties she resumed her studies, that time with Gordon Delamont. With another Delamont student she wrote Lullaby of the Iroquois, based on a poem by Pauline Johnson. The song is now in the British Columbia Board of Education music book.

PHYLLIS MARSHALL

Phyllis Marshall, long one of the top stars of CBC radio and television programs, sang early in her career with Toronto dance bands, including those of Bert Niosi, Cliff McKay and Trump Davidson. A highlight of her career in the late forties was an eight month tour with Cab Calloway's orchestra in the U.S.A. where she later appeared in night clubs as a solo performer. Early in the sixties Miss Marshall toured British cities and appeared on BBC television. In Canada, she was one of the first Canadian performers to appear on television. On radio she starred on several memorable programs: Blues For Friday, Starlight Moods, Percy Faith's Music With Strings. On record, a Columbia LP showcases her voice in a jazz setting created by international jazzmen Buck Clayton and Buddy Tate. On stage, she has appeared in plays, revues and musical comedies.

JACK DUFFY

Jack Duffy is today one of Canada's top variety performers, appearing as an actor and comedian in network TV shows, including Party Game, the George Kirby show, Purple Playhouse, but like many of his colleagues, he, too, sang with the bands. In Duffy's case, he started at the top. Along with George Dean, Ron Martin, Babs Masters and Babs Babineau, a Toronto vocal group called

Jack Duffy (left) when he was host of the CBC's television series, In The Mood, poses with guest star Benny Goodman and the show's band leader, Guido Basso.

The Bob-O-Links, Duffy was hired by Tommy Dorsey when he visited Toronto in 1948. Jack's companions eventually returned to Toronto but he continued to sing with the Dorsey band, replacing regular vocalist Gordon Polk. Duffy toured with Dorsey from August, 1948, to July, 1950, an important period in his life. "Tommy Dorsey was a disciplinarian," he says. "He made you aware, made you dig the music. If you goofed you didn't last long!"

WALLY KOSTER

Wally Koster, who started out in the dance band field in his home town of Winnipeg, came to Toronto to sing with Ellis McLintock's orchestra, and later with Mart Kenney's. From the dance band world it was just a short step to CBC radio and television where Koster soon moved into the top ranks with appearances on Cross Canada Hit Parade, The Big Revue, Matinee Party, On Stage, Mr. Showbusiness and shows of his own. In the early sixties, Wally began making night club appearances and then moved into musical comedy and a variety of stage productions. Among them were Cole Porter's Out Of This World, a series of summer musicals (Guys and Dolls, Carousel and Gentlemen Prefer Blondes, the latter with Jane Morgan), Most Happy Fella at the O'Keefe Centre, and in centennial year Pierre Berton's Paradise Hill at Charlottetown and W.O. Mitchell's Wild Rose in Calgary. Through the years Koster continued to play trombone, as he had in Winnipeg, and which he still does leading his own band in Toronto hotels. He also operates his own booking agency. His voice is often heard in the commercial TV field as an announcer. His singing voice is featured on a Capitol album of Broadway songs.

BABS BABINEAU

Babs Babineau will be forever grateful for the days she spent as a dance band vocalist. "If it hadn't been for Eddie Stroud I'd probably be working in a bank," she says today. Instead Babs, after years of studio work (singing jingles, as a solo voice and group singer in TV plays and documentaries) has acquired a kind of backstage underground reputation. The public may not be aware of her, but everyone in the musical world is. Invariably those in the know praise her "musicianly" singing. As her former boss Eddie Stroud says: "Babs was a natural. Her tuning, her phrasing were out of this world."

Babs sang with Stroud's orchestra for three years, then joined the vocal group, The Bob-O-Links which eventually went on the road with Tommy Dorsey's orchestra for a year. Back in Toronto she appeared on many radio and TV programs in the fifties interspersed with commercial jobs which, by the sixties, almost completely took up her time.

TERRY DALE

Terry Dale began her career as a singer first with Earle Hill's band in her native Vancouver, then with the Art Hallman orchestra in Toronto, but actually she had been singing since the age of four on Vancouver radio stations. When Terry left the Hallman band three years later she went into broadcasting full time, appearing on the Wayne and Shuster shows (both radio and TV), on radio's Happy Motoring Show with Wally Koster, Hotel Down Beat featuring west coast leader Lance Harrison, the Tommy Hunter show and Music 201, hosted by Alan Millar whom she later married. Her TV credits include the big band program, Mallets and Brass, On Stage produced by Norman Jewison, Lucio Agostini's Music Album and an In The Mood show starring bandleader Les Brown. Her own shows have included Terry and Me and the Terry Dale Show out of Vancouver. On stage and in clubs she has appeared in Toronto, Vancouver, Korea and Japan.

Louise King, a featured singer with Ferde Mowry's orchestra, was often heard on the Carl Lucas Hockey Broadcast. Miss King eventually joined Percy Faith's orchestra in Chicago.

Singer Maxine Ware of Winnipeg was featured with Paul Grosney's orchestra when the band played at Rancho Don Carlos from 1949 to 1958.

Norman Harris' orchestra, with vocalist Margaret Henry, in *The King Edward Hotel's Oak Room* in the mid-forties.

BERT NIOSI

Radio offered immense riches to music fans in the thirties. To this day dance band addicts still get dreamy-eyed thinking of the wealth of music on the airwaves.

Part of the fun was staying up until the late hours, picking up stations from all the remote corners of the U.S.A. The big bands of that country quite likely had as many loyal followers in Canada as they had at home.

American programming was picked up as a matter of course by Canadians, but it should be noted that Americans were also listening to Canadian bands. Around 1939, the CBC announced that it had in the previous year featured several Canadian bands, including Mart Kenney, Horace Lapp, Don Turner, Ozzie Williams and Luigi Romanelli in a series of exchange programs with U.S. networks.

For years Luigi Romanelli was presented on CBC stations and the U.S. Blue Network. Trump Davidson, with the band in the mid-thirties, says Romanelli was the first to broadcast on CBS weekly programs. "We also did one from CKGW on the top of the King Edward Hotel. I had to beat it up to the studio to do three or four songs, then back downstairs just in time to sing the first tune with the band." To add to the orchestra's already full program it also appeared on a morning radio show five days a week at eight in the morning!

Bert Niosi's famous little band within the band was actually created for an appearance on a CBC broadcast. It proved so popular on the air that it became a regular attraction along with the full Niosi personnel at the Palais Royale ballroom.

Perhaps the strongest advocate of radio is bandleader Art Hallman, who even before he joined Mart Kenney's Western Gentlemen in Vancouver, was a staff pianist at CJOR. "Radio was the thing," he says. "It made all the artists in Canada. That's how I first came to be known. We used to broadcast, then follow up with a tour. That's what established many Canadian artists."

"My big thrill was listening to radio, listening to the bands of Benny Goodman, Cab Calloway, Glen Gray. There were many bands on the west coast. A whole breed of them up and down the coast. The Loffner-Harris band from San Francisco was on

[1]   The Mart Kenney orchestra in the Alexandra Ballroom during a CJOR broadcast in 1932. The man in front of the tuba is Hec MacCallum. Art Hallman is at the piano.

[2]   Paul Grosney's band, with vocalist Maxine Ware, on Paul's CKRC radio show in Winnipeg.

[3]   Freddy Martin with the band that played at the Cocoanut Grove in the Ambassador Hotel for 20 years. Canadian listeners picked up the band on broadcasts out of Los Angeles.

every night. Harris was Phil Harris, who later led the band on the Jack Benny show. I remember listening to Gus Arnheim when he had Bing Crosby singing with him . . . and Freddy Martin when Merv Griffin was his singer."

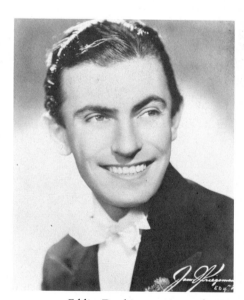

Eddie Duchin, a piano playing bandleader, attracted a huge following with radio broadcasts on Saturday and Sunday afternoons.

When Hallman established his own band, his theme was Just a Moment More With You. Like The West, A Nest And You, Dear, the theme of his former boss, Mart Kenney, it was an immediate identification. The themes are, in fact, to those who heard them way back an instant, nostalgic reminder of the dance band days . . .

WAYNE KING AND HIS ORCHESTRA
STEEL PIER
MAY·30th·1936
1035·K
CENTRAL STUDIOS

1

Sammy Kaye was often heard in Canada on U.S. network programs. Swing and Sway With Sammy Kaye was the famous phrase that introduced the band to radio listeners.

2

Frank Driggs
1   Wayne King's orchestra at the height of its fantastic success in 1936 at Atlantic City's Steel Pier.

Gene Smith photo
2   Jan Garber, who took over the Freddy Large orchestra, a Canadian band that played in the Lombardo style, was often heard on CBS broadcasts on KNX, Los Angeles.

3   Benny Goodman, with his singer Helen Ward, at the Congress Hotel in Chicago, broadcast on station WBBM.

3

Bert Niosi and his men pose before a CFRB microphone way back in the early thirties.

Guy Lombardo and the Royal Canadians broadcasting on WABC.

Gene Smith photo
Ted Weems, who broadcast out of Chicago on WGN, in 1938 featured Marilyn Maxwell, on his right, who became a movie actress, and Perry Como, fifth from the right, a television star of the sixties.

91

Frank Driggs
Vaughn Monroe and his band in a 1942 photo taken at the Meadowbrook in Cedar Grove, N.J. The late bandleader's theme song was Racing With the Moon.

Duke Ellington and His Famous Orchestra in an elaborate ballroom setting in the early thirties. On late night broadcasts, the band captivated thousands of Canadian fans with its theme, East St. Louis Toodle-oo.

When it came to hearing the best of the American big bands, Canadians were fortunate. As next-door neighbours to the U.S.A. Canadian cities were automatically included in the big band tours. It was just as easy for an American band to wend its way northward as it was to go east or west.

In Ontario one dance hall especially favoured by fans and dance bands alike was Dunn's Pavilion. Located in Bala, Ontario, a tiny town in the Muskoka lakes resortland, Dunn's was the perfect setting for a movie with a 1940's background. It still stands but the sounds are different, mostly in the rock mode now and far removed from the days when Howard Cable and Eddie Stroud and Frank Evans led bands there. (Incidentally, the first band to play at Dunn's was Luigi Romanelli; Cable had the honour of opening the second, renovated pavilion in 1941.)

Gerry Dunn who ran the pavilion from 1928 to 1963, still lives in Bala in the summer months, still runs a pharmacy as he did when he was owner, and still admits that yes his pavilion was different from all others. To enter the ballroom, patrons had first to walk through his drug store but that was a happy experience because usually Dunn himself was out front shaking hands and talking with everyone as they came in.

The Pavilion, a magnetic attraction for miles around (music lovers came from North Bay, Parry Sound, Orillia, Toronto, Hamilton, even Buffalo, N.Y.) held up to 2,000 guests, with chairs and tables encircling the dance floor. The stage resembled a small cottage, complete with flower boxes and lamps, an idea Dunn had picked up when he saw a similar setting in a Detroit ballroom.

Unlike most ballroom operators, he booked the visiting bands on a Tuesday or a Wednesday night. As he recalls, "most ballroom operators wanted the big bands on the weekends, but I was always packed anyway."

Apparently the U.S. bands liked the arrangement. They were always certain of huge crowds on those mid-week dates. Among them Dunn notes that Frankie Masters was the first U.S. band to play in the new Pavilion in 1941; the Dorsey Brothers appeared separately and together and sadly it proved to be their last engagement together. Tommy Dorsey died shortly afterward. Of all

An interior view of Dunn's Pavilion in Bala, Ont.

the bands and there were many (including Guy Lombardo, Cab Calloway, Count Basie, Glenn Miller, Billy May, Les Brown, Woody Herman, Hal McIntyre, Duke Ellington) Louis Armstrong brought in the largest crowd in the Pavilion's history. "That was in 1961 and that was the biggest crowd we ever had, before or since. It was so big we had to give money back and people were still standing outside clamouring to get in."

Gerry Dunn, the famous proprietor of the Bala drug store.

Gerry Dunn in front of his service station.

Eddie Stroud plays for the dancers at Dunn's Pavilion.

Dunn's Pavilion as it looked back in the forties.

Les Brown and His Band of Renown frequently visited Canada, especially Dunn's Pavilion in Bala, Ont.

Ben Bernie, "The Ol' Maestro",
and All the Lads were imported from
the U.S.A. to open the Royal York
Hotel in Toronto on June 11, 1929.

Count Basie's orchestra has been appearing in Canadian cities since the thirties. Like Duke Ellington's orchestra, the Basie band still continues to play here, most recently in Toronto at the Royal York Hotel's Imperial Room which still caters to the dancing public.

Gene Smith photo
Woody Herman, a favourite from the forties, still brings his band to Canada. Here he's seen with his 1951 crew at the Casino Ballroom, Catalina Island.

Frank Driggs photo

Harry James' orchestra in a studio session with a very young Dick Haymes shaking the maracas. James commanded the highest price of all the bands that ever played at the Palace Pier.

Gene Smith photo

Historic jazz was made by the Benny Goodman Sextet (that's the legendary Charlie Christian on guitar) wherever it played. This photo dates back to 1940, around the time Goodman appeared at the CNE Tent.

BENNY GOODMAN SEXTET

102

Gene Smith photo
Always popular with Canadians was the Stan Kenton orchestra, shown here in 1951. In the back row, extreme right is Montreal-born Maynard Ferguson who began leading his band in 1957.

Gene Smith photo
Bob Crosby and his orchestra back in 1940 around the time it appeared in Canada. In Toronto that was the Palais Royale.

GUY LOMBARDO

"Who is the most popular bandleader to come out of Canada?" The question is unfair. Guy Lombardo and His Royal Canadians have topped the list since they left for the United States in the twenties.

Guy and his brothers, Carmen, Lebert and Victor, all natives of London, Ontario, arrived at a style that became known as "The sweetest music this side of heaven." Maybe the tunes have changed, but the style? Never.

That Lombardo sound has given its leader and his men some of the highest salaries in the dance band business. It has given the band a following that reaches epic proportions every New Year's Eve when it plays to millions on its traditional TV broadcast. It's a band that had been ridiculed and lampooned, yet it moves ever forward on its unswerving course. What Lombardo fans like about it is its relentless beat, perfect for dancing. If ever there was a dance band in the full sense of the word this is it.

Guy, a shrewd and likeable business man, attributes the orchestra's success to his father. "I think our early training was very important," he said on a trip to Toronto. "We were taught to be studious, law abiding citizens. We practised hard at our music. He had three or four boys taking lessons and money was hard to come by. He wasn't going to have them wasting it.

"He was very responsible for what started our success. He used to say to us 'always give a little bit more than they ask for.' I am proud that we have never played an engagement that we haven't been invited back. Year after year we get invitations, but I think that's because of our Canadian training. I have seen it in other Canadians who have come to the United States. They give more than they have to."

The Lombardo brothers have been so successful and so popular in the United States and Canada that it's a surprise to realize that they have never ventured beyond the North American continent. Offers have come from England, from Europe, from Russia and the far East, but somehow the band never seems to have time.

For one thing, the Lombardos have other interests. In the

summer, Guy and the Canadians spend their time at Jones Beach, on Long Island's south shore, where they appear in lavish musicals to huge audiences.

For the remainder of the year, the Royal Canadians are on the road. The dance band business may have gone into a decline in the forties but don't tell that to the Lombardo brothers from London, Ontario.

BILLY BISSETT

A Canadian bandleader of the thirties who won considerable recognition in England was Billy Bissett. By the mid-forties, then known as Billy Bishop, he was attracting fans in the United States.

Bissett's career began as a youngster in St. Catharines where he organized a high school band and during a summer holiday took it on a tour through the New England states, ending up in New York City. The nervy youngsters hoped to make it big and surprisingly enough they did, but not in the way they expected. They hired an audition hall and asked all the orchestra booking agents to attend. Fortunately, for them, among the agents was a MCA representative who was actually looking for an all-Canadian band to follow the Abe Lyman orchestra into the Kit Kat Club. Billy and the boys got the job.

MCA had booked another of its bands, led by Ben Bernie to follow Bissett's band into the Kit Kat which turned out to be a coincidental event. Ben Bernie had just left Toronto where his orchestra had been the first American outfit to play at the new Royal York Hotel in June, 1929.

Eventually Bissett himself was to appear at the Royal York but only after some success in the United States. After the Kit Kat engagement the band was booked by MCA to play in Syracuse, Cleveland; to tour with Fox Vaudeville, then returned to Canada.

Bissett's first Toronto appearance took place at the Silver Slipper in November, 1930, with Duart MacLean, who had been a former co-leader, with Bissett playing lead alto. (Later MacLean formed his own band and went into the Old Mill.)

From September, 1933, to January, 1936, the band appeared regularly at the Royal York Hotel, then returned to England and appearances at the Savoy Hotel, the Mayfair, the Cafe de Paris in London, and the Royal Bath Hotel in Bournemouth until September, 1939, when World War II broke out. Toronto bandleader Doug Kemp (he led his own band at Masonic Auditorium during the fifties) who played saxophone in the Bissett orchestra said it was a good hotel band, one that was also featured in British films

Dinner at the Ritz, The Divorce of Lady X and The Sidewalks of London.

In 1940 Bissett moved to the United States, organized a band, and then under the name Billy Bishop spent the next few years working out of Chicago. In 1953 Billy gave up the band business and became a stock broker in Beverly Hills, California. Now in retirement, he lives in San Diego, with his wife, the former Alice Mann who was vocalist with his band before and after their marriage in 1937.

Billy Bishop, originally Billy Bissett, with his American band in the forties. His vocalist is his wife, Alice Mann.

GLEN GRAY

Dozens of Canadian dance bands played at Toronto's Casa Loma in the thirties and forties but none ever achieved the recognition given to the Orange Blossoms, the first American orchestra to play there.

The Orange Blossoms had been contracted to appear at the great castle on the hill to bring in customers in 1927. At that time, the castle, built between 1911 and 1914 by Sir Henry Mill Pellatt, had been taken over by the city and turned into a hotel.

The American band, assembled by Detroit bandleader Jean Goldkette, who had half a dozen bands under his name on the road, arrived at the castle and stayed eight months. Its leader was a trumpeter named Hank Biagini, but it was the alto saxist, Spike Knoblaugh, who was to become even better known.

Ed Culley, of the well known Culley family, was a member of that original Casa Loma band, along with Torontonians Kirt Little, trumpet; Charles Hayward, guitar, and saxophonist Joe Bernstein. "But when they went to the United States we stayed here," said Culley, who played alto saxophone. "They wanted only U.S. musicians."

Back in the States even the American musicians couldn't find jobs. By 1929 Goldkette gave up his career as a band leader and the Orange Blossoms were on their own. Spurred on by Knoblaugh the men accepted some one night stands through New England, and eventually landed in New York where they played at the Roseland Ballroom. There they were known as Goldkette's Casa Loma Orchestra. Maybe it was the name, but more likely it was the band's style (a big band jazz style) that caught the public's attention.

Arrangements by Gene Gifford were the backbone of the band's style. That helped a lot and so, too, did the new leader. In New York, the musicians had voted to have the tall, handsome Knoblaugh take over the band. His name in full was actually Glen Gray Knoblaugh.

When in 1933 the band had become known as the Casa Loma Orchestra (Goldkette's name by then had been deleted) it was decided that it would be better to promote the band as Glen Gray and the Casa Loma Orchestra. (Musicians who worked in the band at that time recall that for a while the term, Casa Loma Orchestra, was confusing people. It wasn't unusual to have dancers come up to the stand and ask for Mr. Casa Loma.)

From then on, the Casa Loma band was never out of work. Glen Gray continued as leader until 1947. A year or two before he died in 1963 he returned to Toronto for a TV appearance and still maintained that the castle on the hill had been one of the most pleasant places he had ever played.

GLEN GRAY and the CASA LOMA ORCHESTRA
featuring Kenny Sargent, "Pee Wee" Hunt and Sonny Dunham

Exclusive Management ROCKWELL-O'KEEFE, Inc. 9028 SUNSET BLVD. HOLLYWOOD, CALIF. 32 W. RANDOLPH ST. CHICAGO, ILL. R.K.O. BUILDING. RADIO CITY. NEW YORK, N.Y.

Glen Gray and the Casa Loma orchestra. In the personnel were Kenny Sargent, Pee Wee Hunt and Sonny Dunham.

Glen Gray and the Casa Loma Orchestra in the thirties.

GLEN GRAY and His Original
CASA LOMA
Orchestra

DENNY VAUGHAN

When Denny Vaughan went overseas early in World War II he was unknowingly already on his way to international fame. Born in Toronto where he had studied music at the University of Toronto he began his musical career as a singer and pianist. In years to come he was a dance band leader, the first ever to appear at Montreal's Queen Elizabeth Hotel, a composer, arranger and musical director on Hollywood television shows.

Before he was to wjn acclaim in England, Denny had already started conducting a dance band, at the age of 15, in Toronto. He played piano with his orchestra, and also sang when he couldn't afford to hire a vocalist. While still in high school he worked for several months as singer-pianist with Horace Lapp's Royal York Hotel band, but at 19 Denny's world changed. It was then he became a member of the Canadian Armed Forces, went overseas and discovered when he stayed on in England after the war, that he was the idol of teenagers.

His records were such huge sellers that he became known as Britain's Frank Sinatra. In the fifties when Denny returned to Canada, he became the idol of Canadian teenagers, only then he was known as Canada's Perry Como. Around that time Vaughan voiced a rather wistful wish that he might become known as just Denny Vaughan.

Back in Canada, Denny won even more popularity when he starred on his own CBC radio and TV shows, at the same time working behind the scenes in the publishing and recording fields.

In 1958 Denny took his orchestra into the Queen Elizabeth Hotel. Then, in the sixties, again attained international stature when he moved to Hollywood. For five years he worked as bandleader and choral director on the Glen Campbell Hour, the Smothers Brothers Show and the Pat Paulsen program.

When Moxie Whitney left the Royal York Hotel's Imperial Room in 1971 it was expected that Denny Vaughan, by then returned from Hollywood, would take his place. Instead Denny returned to Montreal where he worked in and around the city for a year. Only 50 years old, he died a year later, on October 2, 1972.

Denny Vaughan at the piano with Richard Avonde's orchestra at the Brant Inn in 1941. In the front row, second from right is Jack Kane, who became nationally known for his CBC orchestra.

INDEX

TO THE PHOTOGRAPHS...